HOW-TO SERIES

for the HR Professional

Documenting
Job
Content

Thomas J. Hackett, CCP, CBP
Valerie C. Williams

About WorldatWork*

WorldatWork is the world's leading not-for-profit professional association dedicated to knowledge leadership in compensation, benefits and total rewards. Founded in 1955, WorldatWork focuses on human resources disciplines associated with attracting, retaining and motivating employees. Besides serving as the membership association of the professions, the WorldatWork family of organizations provides education, certification (Certified Compensation Professional — CCP*, Certified Benefits Professional — CBP™ and Global Remuneration Professional — GRP*), publications, knowledge resources, surveys, conferences, research and networking. WorldatWork Society of Certified Professionals and Alliance for Work-Life Progress (AWLP) are part of the WorldatWork family.

The Professional Association for Compensation, Benefits and Total Rewards

WorldatWork
14040 N. Northsight Blvd., Scottsdale, AZ 85260
480/951-9191   Fax 480/483-8352
www.worldatwork.org

Publishing Manager: Dan Cafaro
Graphic Design: Mark Anthony Muñoz
Production Manager: Rebecca Williams Ficker
Staff Contributor: Bonnie Serino

Table of Contents

Overview

The world of work is changing. In the past, a single job was a small piece of a very large puzzle. Now, the puzzle is being cut into larger blocks, with less emphasis on the individual pieces. Alternative reward systems, total quality management initiatives and drastically changing demographics have shifted the focus from the traditional approach of analyzing a single job to looking at groups of jobs to determine how they add value in the process of producing a product or service, and how they can be shared by more than one worker. Consequently, the view of work has broadened to include how workers interrelate to add value (teams). Work is further complicated by some pieces of the work flow shifting to an external work force as pieces are "outsourced" to outside vendors. This booklet provides a methodology for analyzing and documenting work, and it incorporates workflow analysis techniques.

Job analysis is the process of determining and defining the content of jobs. Traditionally, when a job was viewed as a discrete unit of work, it was documented in a single job description. Today's broader view, called "work analysis," includes all of those job incumbents within the organization, directly engaged in or having input to a specific segment of producing a product or service.

By shifting the focus from a single piece of the puzzle to the big picture, many organizations report increased quality, efficiency and morale. However, reorientation and retraining of workers often is required.

To understand how the process works today and to determine how it can be improved, job and work analysis must be conducted. Traditional methods of single-job analysis (i.e., observation, interviews and questionnaires) not only are useful tools in determining what is being done, how it is being done and who is doing it, but also they are useful in conducting work analysis.

Work analysis is the study of the human element involved in the creation of a product or service. It usually follows the process from raw material to customer usage to understand how individuals or groups of workers together add value. Because the marketplace is demanding greater quality products and on-demand services, work analysis often is conducted in reverse, tracing a quality problem from customer identification to the source in the creation process.

Legislative Considerations

Job and work analysis always have been affected by federal, state and local legislative considerations such as Equal Pay, Equal Employment Opportunity (EEO) and Affirmative Action. (In Canada, pay-equity legislation in many jurisdictions calls for careful job analysis. Those responsible are advised to consult with the Provincial Ministry.)

More recently, the Americans with Disabilities Act (ADA) is affecting work analysis substantially. Effective July 26, 1992, ADA requires employers to identify "essential job functions," which are those fixed parts of a defined job that cannot be reassigned easily to other workers. Essential job functions are performed by employees who do not have impairments that would prevent them from performing these functions.

Once essential job functions are identified, the employer must consider "reasonable accommodations" that will enable an otherwise qualified person who has one or more impairments to perform the essential job functions. "Essential job functions" and "reasonable accommodations" have to be determined on a case-by-case basis. As a result, ADA has created a renewed interest among affected employers (with 25 or more employees) in job analysis because it is the beginning point for these determinations. Because job analysis is also the foundation for content-based job evaluation, and in turn job evaluation usually is followed by the development of formal salary structures, readers are encouraged to study these issues as well.

What Is a Job?

In practice, the terms "job" and "position" often are interchanged. However, there is a difference. A job consists of a collection of duties and responsibilities, which can be further divided into specific tasks and further into task elements (Figure 1). Using an "executive assistant" job as an example, a task element is the simple motion of inserting a piece of paper into a typewriter. A task is typing the minutes of a particular meeting. A duty is having to maintain a record of those minutes from a series of meetings. A responsibility of this job is having account-ability for the recording, typing, dissemination and maintenance of the record. When there are enough duties and responsibilities to require the employment of a worker, a position exists. Consequently, an organization has as many positions as it has current workers and job openings (vacancies). When more than one worker is employed in the same or similar position(s), a job exists.

For example, when two workers are employed as administrative assistants, and their duties and responsibilities are essentially the same, there are two administrative assistant positions but only one administrative assistant job. Of course, there are also single-incumbent jobs (for example, the chief executive officer). Jobs that are common to many organizations are known as occupations. For example, most organizations employ administrative assistants and accountants; thus, both are occupations.

A work group or team exists when a worker interacts with others to produce a component of a product or service for sale or consumption (Figure 2). The emphasis is on the human element involved in the production, not the mechanical or automated processes involved, except to understand how the worker interacts with or affects them. The focus of work analysis is on how worker interactions add value during the process. It consequently serves as the first step in identifying teams. Single-job analysis actually can be part of work analysis, depending on the ultimate objective of the analysis project. Job or work analysis is a step-by-step process.

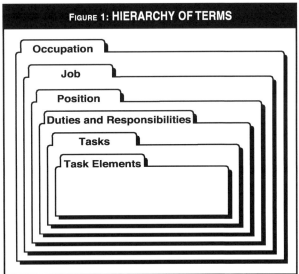

Figure 1: HIERARCHY OF TERMS

Occupation
Job
Position
Duties and Responsibilities
Tasks
Task Elements

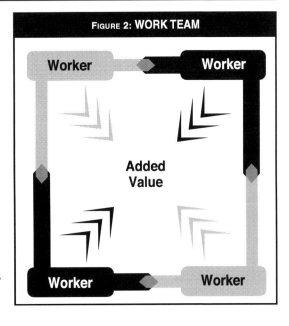

Figure 2: WORK TEAM

Worker

Worker

Added Value

Worker

Worker

1

Obtain Management Approval

Before beginning a major undertaking in any organization, be sure to obtain top management support. The human resources department should not initiate a job analysis effort unilaterally.

Support is won more easily when management is aware of its legal liabilities under the Fair Labor Standards Act (FLSA), ADA, Equal Pay and all the various local, state and federal civil rights laws (in Canada, the Human Rights Act and pay-equity laws). Consequently, it may be necessary first to educate management about the critical role job analysis has in minimizing liability under these laws. Job analysis also is the first step to ensure that jobs are classified properly as either exempt or nonexempt, that "essential job functions" are identified, and that hiring requirements (i.e., job specifications) are clear and defensible. Moreover, performance appraisals can lead to lawsuits under state and federal anti-discrimination laws. Legally, a performance appraisal is a type of selection procedure or employment test. The basis for developing standards of performance is the job description, which is developed from a detailed job analysis. Consequently, job analysis is critical to developing a sound performance management system.

When coupled with work analysis, there are many aspects of job analysis that also are of interest to management. All organizations want to ensure that roles and responsibilities are clearly understood, that there is no duplication of effort, and that work flows smoothly and efficiently from one department or function to another. In an era when organizations are seeking to achieve the "right" size, job and work analysis also can establish the basis on which staffing decisions can be made. Technology has greatly impacted the design of work and efficiency of workers. An up-to-date job analysis ensures management that job content, job descriptions, and so on accurately reflect how work is being performed and what skills are required. It also ensures them that correct job matching occurs when benchmark jobs are priced against relevant labor markets. Job analysis is also is necessary to develop a successful training program for workers assigned to jobs that require formal training. Job and work analysis give management a clear picture of who is doing (or not doing) what, and they provide the basis for ensuring that the company's limited compensation dollars are properly spent.

To institute effective quality management programs, it is imperative that the work dynamics be understood before any realistic improvements can be made. However, management's desire to make things better is not enough; employee acceptance also is needed.

2

Gain Employee Acceptance

Employee acceptance is crucial. If management has done an inadequate job of communicating what the job analysis or work-study effort is all about and the reasons for it, negative employee relations may result.

Because of the recent downsizing trend in American business, employees naturally will view job or work analysis efforts with suspicion. To mitigate any negative impact of the job analysis process, an upbeat communication campaign should be developed to explain to employees why the study is being done (e.g., implementation of an incentive program, compliance with ADA, re-evaluation of jobs, development of the strategic plan, development of total quality management programs, etc.).

Emphasize the benefits to the employee as well — a clearly defined job that will be the basis for developing performance standards and evaluating the job's worth, or the creation of opportunities for employee participation in the production process to increase quality and efficiency, and to enhance employee satisfaction. Potentially, the study could result in determination of required competencies and training developed for employees in those competencies that employees might now fall below new standards. The latter may particularly be the case with new/upgraded technology. Communicate how employees can help the process by filling out questionnaires properly, responding to interview questions with detailed information, making suggestions for work improvement and identifying problem areas.

Emphasize to employees how critical it is to get good information about their jobs. If the job-analysis effort is the first step in a project to re-evaluate jobs, the organization should promise to communicate the results — consistent with management's philosophy on communicating compensation matters. To maintain credibility in the future, it is imperative to honor that promise. (For more information, see *Communicating Compensation Programs*, another booklet published by the WorldatWork.)

If the work-study is intended to result in a realignment of workers into teams or to implement quality improvements, explain to participants that their input at the outset is vital, and that the final work redesign plan will be presented to them first for their suggestions. Employees must believe that their participation is welcome and will make a difference.

> # Employees must believe that their participation is welcome and will make a difference.

Gaining Union Support

In a union environment, gaining the union's cooperation and support is always important. However, even without that support, management has the right to collect important information about jobs. Fortunately, union support frequently is forthcoming because job-analysis information is helpful in defining jobs in contracts and in conducting pay surveys. However, job descriptions sometimes become work "rules" and handcuff management's flexibility in union environments.

Work-studies may be opposed if a union perceives it to be the first step in job eliminations. However, in today's competitive, global economy, unions understand the need for efficiency and quality. It is on this basis that their cooperation can be solicited, especially if they are invited to participate in the process so everyone is working toward a common goal — a profitable and stable organization that produces a quality product.

3

Decide Who Will
Conduct the Analysis

J ob or work analysis can be performed by anyone in the organization who has been trained or who is familiar with the work being analyzed. Of course, it is always best to ask trained job analysts from the human resources department or elsewhere to conduct the study. This is not always practical, however, due to time constraints, geographic limitations or company size.

To be efficient, especially when many jobs need to be analyzed, organizations ask supervisors, job incumbents, human resources staff, outside consultants and others to perform the analysis. The best results come from directly involving supervisors and incumbents. Most important, mutual concern for working efficiently and enhanced communication between worker and manager often result. If everyone is not trained in the analysis techniques discussed in this booklet, the results will be inconsistent and, consequently, of limited value.

Whoever is chosen to do the analysis should have good interpersonal skills, good writing skills and knowledge of how the organization functions. In addition, successful analysts will be inquisitive by nature and objective in their business dealings.

4

Think in Terms
of Work Flow

In all organizations, whether profit or nonprofit, public or private, work "flows" from one area to another (Figure 3). Whether it is manual or intellectual work that is being analyzed, think of work flow in these terms: The worker will receive work from someone (or somewhere), will add value by doing something to it and then will pass it on to the next worker. If no value is added (this may frequently be the case, particularly in bureaucratic organizations), the activity should be reviewed to determine the implications of discontinuing it. If it is discontinued, the worker should be reassigned, if possible.

In a quality management environment, workflow focuses heavily on the "added-value" component. Workflow on an assembly line, for example, might involve one worker passing a semi-finished product to the next worker on the line, who adds another part and then passes it on, and so on until completion.

In quality management, workflow is scrutinized from two standpoints:

- ## From within the job itself

- ## Through the entire process of the work flow

Workflow is not simply lateral. In knowledge work, workers receive a project assignment from their bosses, or a request from another department, or a report from a subordinate. A job analyst's concern is what the worker does with the assignment. Therefore, workflow can be vertical (work assignments are passed upward or downward in the organization), lateral (work assignments are received from and sent to peer departments), or diagonal (work is requested from or sent to incumbents who are in other functions and at different levels in the organizational hierarchy). Often, the formal chain of command is not followed, and workflow speed increases; this is important to remember in conducting work flow analysis, especially if the ultimate goal of the analysis is to reorganize job incumbents into teams.

While review of workflow is important for both quality management and job evaluation purposes, the process differs for each purpose. For job evaluation, it is important to understand a specific job and its relationship with other jobs in the job-worth hierarchy (the value organizations place on individual jobs). In quality management, workflow is scrutinized from two standpoints:

- **From within the job itself,** by having the job incumbent ask questions for each activity, such as: From where or from whom does the work come? Are there any changes in how the work is provided to me that would make my job easier or faster? How could I enhance the work I

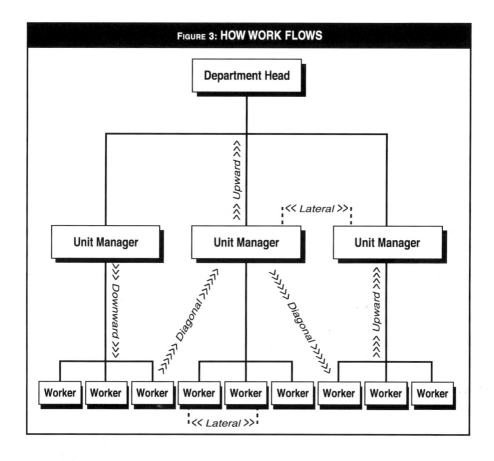

FIGURE 3: HOW WORK FLOWS

provide to others to expedite the next step in the work flow? By asking such questions, the worker is trained to think in an analytical way about what is being done and why.

- **Through the entire process of the work flow,** to determine if a major activity can be accomplished more effectively and efficiently through reassignment or through modification of one or more tasks or responsibilities, not only across job functions but also across departmental lines. If the purpose of the work study ultimately is to enhance teamwork, the analysis will focus additionally on identifying the best cluster of workers, or "team," that adds value to the product or service being produced.

5

Consult Secondary
Sources First

B efore beginning to conduct the actual job or work analysis by approaching a worker or a supervisor, it is always useful to study existing secondary-source information about the job or process to be reviewed. There are many sources of information already available about the work being performed. Figure 4 shows typical secondary sources.

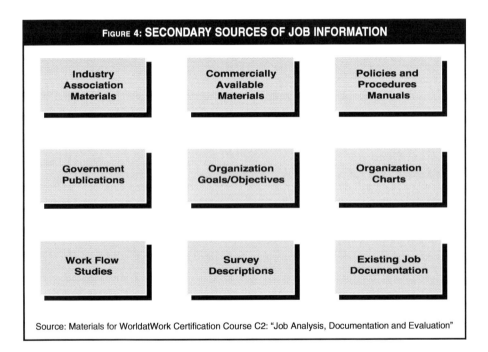

FIGURE 4: SECONDARY SOURCES OF JOB INFORMATION

Industry Association Materials	Commercially Available Materials	Policies and Procedures Manuals
Government Publications	Organization Goals/Objectives	Organization Charts
Work Flow Studies	Survey Descriptions	Existing Job Documentation

Source: Materials for WorldatWork Certification Course C2: "Job Analysis, Documentation and Evaluation"

Internal Sources

The most obvious and perhaps most useful piece of information available is the existing job description. Instead of starting from scratch, it is possible simply to update the job description based on additional information gathered from the job incumbent, supervisor or both. Focus on "what has changed" rather than re-writing the job description from the beginning. Again, technology has greatly influenced how work is done, and it is imperative that these changes are captured through a current job analysis. Generic job descriptions provided in salary surveys of benchmark jobs are another good secondary source of information.

Other sources can offer quite a bit of information about the job, about the unit in which the job or work group is located and about work flow. In terms of workflow, the most useful source is the organization chart. It tells where the worker function is located within the organization, and it provides a good idea of where the work comes from and where it goes after the unit has added value.

Many organizations design company phone books that reflect their structure. For example, the head of a department is shown at the top of the page, indented below is a list of the major functional units within that department, and further indented are the specific names and titles of workers in each unit. When current formal organization charts are not available, the phone book can be a valuable substitute, but keep in mind that it may not reflect actual reporting relationships accurately.

Today's organizations often use the management-by-objectives (MBO) approach to communicate the key contributions expected from each department on an annual basis. These usually are broken into specific objectives for each worker, and they will indicate the expected contribution(s) of the job being analyzed. Organization or department strategic plans and annual budget write-ups also can provide helpful, though indirect, information. These are important models to use while conducting the "reality test" in Step 10.

In an attempt to understand which functions can be automated, systems analysts often prepare work studies and procedures manuals. To do so, they will ask job incumbents to keep diaries and logs for a period of time. Certain types of work need to be performed in an orderly and consistent manner, and many organizations develop training or procedures manuals that instruct the worker on how to perform specific tasks. These documents all should be consulted to gain an understanding of the nature of the work that is being performed before actually conducting a job analysis. If parts of the workflow have been "outsourced", the outsourcing contract will usually contain specific "Service Level Agreements" which spell out in detail the work to be performed and the level of quality to be achieved by the external entity.

External Sources

Source material also may be found in government publications, books, magazines and other material published by industry or professional trade associations. The Dictionary of Occupational Titles (DOT), published by the federal government, provides information on more than 20,000 job titles. The government also publishes The Occupational Outlook Handbook, which is cross-referenced to the DOT and provides extensive information about jobs and the outlook for related careers. Both are valuable sources and especially are useful when the analyst has little knowledge of the jobs to be studied. Both DOT and OOH are accessible online.

In addition, many professions such as law, accounting and human resources have associations that gladly will supply information about the nature of work performed by their membership, including model job descriptions. Usually, they also publish magazines and newsletters that, although technical or narrow, certainly can provide valuable insight to a job analyst. In addition, do not forget the local bookstore or library, where information can be found about the type of work that is to be analyzed, including textbooks in the subject field.

Figure 4 is not an exhaustive list. The idea is to use any or all of these sources, as necessary, to gain at least a general understanding of the job before moving to the next step. Moreover, the customer may be the most critical source of information regarding the quality or lack of it that represents the outcome of the work performed.

6

Decide Method and Collect Data

When deciding how to collect the information needed to analyze work, it is important to take into account the scope of the project and the time, staff and costs involved. There are three methods of collecting information about jobs: observation, interviews and questionnaires. Each has advantages and disadvantages (Figure 5).

FIGURE 5: METHODS OF COLLECTING DATA			
Method	**Types of Jobs**	**Advantages**	**Disadvantages**
Observation	Production	Simple, Inexpensive	May be insufficient, time consuming
Interview	All	Thorough	Time consuming, most expensive
Questionnaire	All	Least expensive	Requires followup

Observation

The observation method is most appropriate for manual and repetitive production work. For example, in the case of an assembly line worker attaching simple handles to pieces of equipment, two or three observations would be sufficient to learn where the work comes from, what the assembler does with it and where the work goes after the operation is complete. In-depth questioning of the worker, or having the worker maintain a detailed log for several days, would not be necessary to understand what is being done and how it is being done. For a more complicated or protracted process, it might be necessary to observe several cycles or to observe them piecemeal. The cycles may occur over days or weeks, so it is important to know if the entire function or just part of it is being observed.

How to Observe

Do not assume that the worker knows why the observation is occurring. Remember, the best job analysis occurs in an atmosphere of trust. Once the observation begins, be as unobtrusive as possible so as not to interfere with the process. While observing production jobs, it is important to be aware of the effort the worker exerts in doing the job and the physical environment in which the work is performed. Record noise, heat, moving machine parts, and the weight of parts or equipment handled. Pay special attention to the work environment, e.g., heat, noise, etc. If the work is performed outside, weather and other factors may also be important. Note any exposure or handling of hazardous materials, safety equipment required as well as the physical demand on the worker, for example, ability to lift objects weighing more than 50 pounds. Thank the worker when finished with the observations. It is always a good idea to discuss observations with a supervisor. Summarize any notes taken soon after the observation so important details are not forgotten. If complete, notes are a form of job documentation, even though they usually are developed into a more formal job description.

The observation method is not limited to single-job analysis. It is useful in following a product or service from raw material to finished product, especially if the process is predominantly manual in nature. In fact, it is a valuable first step in total quality management to walk through the entire production process before any changes are contemplated. "Walk-throughs" are also a valuable step when the purpose of the study is to identify appropriate members of work teams.

Observation and Interviews

Observation can be used in conjunction with questionnaires by having workers complete them before observation of the production process. When observing a more sophisticated process, ask the worker a few questions to clarify the observations. For example, suppose an assembler sometimes opens the casing before attaching the handle and makes some adjustment to the internal mechanisms. Observation in this case does not tell the whole story. It is necessary to ask the assembler why the adjustments are being made to some machines and not others, what the adjustment actually is, and how long the average adjustment takes. In a workflow study; ask what could have been done in a previous operation to make the worker's job more efficient, or what the worker could do to streamline the next operation in the process. Try not to interfere with the worker or the process; questioning between cycles is best. If it seems that part of the picture is missing, talk to a supervisor.

Observations: Advantages and Disadvantages

Observation is time-consuming and costly, and it requires observers to be trained properly. By itself, it may not be a sufficient approach to job analysis because the observer might "miss" something important. In a more thorough work analysis, an analyst will have to question why things are being done. Consequently, the analyst will have to discuss his or her observations with a worker's supervisor or other technical experts. While it can be expensive, observation is not as costly as the next method, one-on-one interviewing.

One-on-One Interviewing

The observation method becomes less useful toward the higher end of the organization hierarchy. Watching a financial analyst poring over numbers or executing a computer program will not tell much about what actually is being done, nor will it indicate the skills required to do it. An in-depth discussion with the job incumbent will provide information about what is being done, how and why. A useful analogy often has been drawn between a job analyst doing an interview and a newspaper reporter whose job is to find out who, what, where, when, why and how. As mentioned before, consult secondary sources first to ensure that interview questions are informed and insightful.

Remember, the best interview occurs in an atmosphere of trust and mutual commitment to fact-finding.

Starting an Interview

The most important part of the interview is the beginning (Figure 6). It is always important to put the job incumbent at ease by engaging in informal chitchat to break the ice. Then, as the formal part of the interview begins, it is imperative to explain why the meeting is taking place, what will be discussed and what will occur after the interview is over. If the job incumbent still seems unsure of why the interview is taking

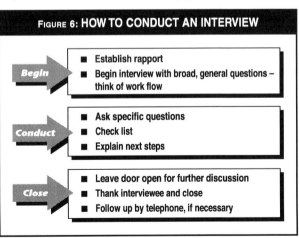

FIGURE 6: HOW TO CONDUCT AN INTERVIEW

Begin
- Establish rapport
- Begin interview with broad, general questions – think of work flow

Conduct
- Ask specific questions
- Check list
- Explain next steps

Close
- Leave door open for further discussion
- Thank interviewee and close
- Follow up by telephone, if necessary

place, it is even more important to provide an adequate explanation. Otherwise, the interviewee will be guarded and the interview will be difficult. Remember, the best interview occurs in an atmosphere of trust and mutual commitment to fact-finding.

Start the actual interview with broad, general questions: On what do you spend most of your time? What are your major responsibilities, from the most important to the least important?

If there are no up-to-date organization charts, start by asking the incumbent to describe the department and the chain of command. Keeping the concept of work flow in mind, probe from the general to the specific as the incumbent begins to answer questions. Listen actively by nodding when the incumbent emphasizes certain points. Use eye-to-eye contact frequently and ask insightful and clarifying questions; it demonstrates genuine interest in the job.

Learn to listen "between the lines." Avoid closed-ended questions that can be answered with simple "yes" or "no" answers. The mission is to obtain as much information about the job as possible.

Writing a Job Description

If the goal is to write a job description from the interview that will be used for job evaluation, it is necessary to know beforehand what the evaluators will be looking for in the job description — that is, what "compensable factors" they will be using to evaluate the job. Compensable factors are ones for which an organization is willing to pay. The specific factors and how they are measured should be explained in the job-evaluation plan being used.

It is important to have a solid understanding of the compensable factors in order to ask pertinent questions or to probe deeper for clarification. Let's take a compensable factor such as "freedom to act," for example, and assume it is measured by the degree of sign-off authority an incumbent has. In the interview, ask: "What is your expenditure approval authority? Is it $1,000? $10,000? $1 million?"

Note that the answer to this question is expressed in numbers, or dimensions. "Dimensions" are statistics that help quantify the scope of the job and the impact that the incumbent performing it has on the bottom line. Frequently requested dimensions include dollar sign-off authority, number of subordinates reporting, budget, dollar-value of plant and equipment, sales volume, revenues, expenses, assets under management, and so on.

Some organizations are moving toward defining jobs in terms of "competencies," the technical and behavioral skills inherently needed to perform the job well. Competencies focus on what people are or can do; they identify traits, knowledge, skills and abilities.

How to Ask Questions

Not all questions will be direct or specific. Figure 7 gives a list of suggested questions that can be modified to create a specific checklist that ensures all important topics have been covered. With practice, it is possible to develop a reliable list of questions and a sequence for asking them. Remember to ask questions that pertain to quality management and work flow. (See questions 9 through 14 in Figure 7.)

Each interview is unique, and some will be easier (and more interesting) than others. Do not try to hold the job incumbent to a preset notion of the order in which things should be discussed. Remember to direct the interview,

---

FIGURE 7: SUGGESTED INTERVIEW QUESTIONS

1. To whom do you report?
2. Who reports to you?
3. What are your budget accountabilities — both budget dollars and the value of assets under your control?
4. What are your principal duties and responsibilities?
5. What is the most important task you perform?
6. How do you spend most of your time?
7. Who do you rely on for information necessary to do your job?
8. Who do you routinely provide information to?
9. What tasks should be completed before the work comes to you?
10. What do you do to add to the quality of the product (or service)?
11. What tasks do you feel are redundant or unnecessary?
12. How can work flow be improved?
13. How would you change the work flow to expedite the process without decreasing quality?
14. What could be handled differently to reduce expenses or costs?
15. Are there any formal guidelines, regulations, policies, etc., that you must follow in fulfilling your job responsibilities?
16. About what decisions would you consult or notify your boss before taking action?
17. How does this job challenge your creativity and problem-solving abilities?
18. With whom do you have regular contact, both inside and outside the organization? What is the reason for the contact?
19. What qualifications would your replacement need, in terms of knowledge and experience, to perform your job at a competent level?
20. Describe the physical conditions in which you work (if appropriate).
21. How would you answer the question, "Why does my job exist?"

---

not control it. A free-flowing dialogue can reveal much. However, to make sure all important issues have been explored, double-check the question list toward the end of the interview.

During the interview, it is acceptable to admit that something is unclear. Every profession has its jargon and acronyms, and professionals often talk in "code," forgetting that the uninitiated do not understand. When unsure of something, stop the interviewee and ask, "What does that mean?", or, "Could you please explain?" Also ask for examples. If a financial analyst talks about a complicated report, ask to see a copy of it. Being able to touch the report physically to see how lengthy and involved it is (or is not) will provide a more complete picture of the work as well as the knowledge, skills and abilities required to do it.

Most organizations separate the responsibility for job analysis from the responsibility for job evaluation.

Closing the Interview

Closing the interview is as important as beginning it. Explain the next steps in the process. (For example, a draft of the job description will be prepared and sent for the incumbent's review and comments within five business days.) Give the incumbent a business card and invite him or her to call if there is anything that should have been discussed but was not. Find out when the best time is to contact the job incumbent with follow-up questions, if necessary.

Most organizations separate the responsibility for job analysis from the responsibility for job evaluation. However, someone in the awkward position of being both analyst and evaluator should not be forced during the interview into giving an indication of the evaluation. Emphasize the current fact-finding role; explain that evaluation decisions will be postponed until the job description is finished and can be reviewed in the context of the larger picture. If the interview was conducted as part of a work-study, explain that the job and the value it adds will be assessed when the whole process has been analyzed.

Often, the incumbent will find that the interview was a valuable experience. Don't be surprised if the incumbent says afterward, "You know, I never stopped to think about how much I actually get involved with around here."

When finished with the interview, take time immediately to summarize and organize notes, especially if there is more than one interview a day or if a time lapse of a day or two is expected before it is possible to write the job description or work-analysis report. Time has a way of eroding the understanding and recall of important details.

Group Interviews

Interviewing is not limited to a single job incumbent. It is possible to conduct a "group interview," where several incumbents are interviewed at the same time. The guidelines presented earlier apply. At times, especially in total-quality programs, it may be desirable to bring several experts from different disciplines together to discuss the work, usually because it is highly technical.

For example, consider an assembler who has to stop occasionally to make an adjustment before attaching the handle. Perhaps there is a problem with the previous operation. By bringing the supervisor, quality-control manager and parts department together, the problem can be identified and resolved. If not, at least there will be an adequate explanation made of why the adjustment is necessary on some machines but not every machine, and a conclusion can be drawn that there is nothing more to be done to prevent it at this time. Such meetings are known as "technical interviews" because they tend to focus on very specific items. Technical interviews are critical in a total-quality study because they help enhance communications, clarify the source of problems and identify possible solutions.

Interviewing Customers

Although a different set of questions may be used to interview customers, the questioning techniques will be similar. However, more emphasis will be placed on product quality and customer needs and wants.

Interviewing: Advantages and Disadvantages

Interviewing is the most costly method of job and work analysis, especially when there are many jobs to be analyzed. For one thing, interviewing occupies two people simultaneously in a single-job analysis, or several in a technical interview or quality review. For another, interviewing takes a lot of time.

Interviewing can be inefficient if the analyst and the interviewee(s) are ill prepared to engage in a meaningful discussion of the work. This can happen if the purpose of the meeting is not explained adequately, if the analyst does not consult secondary sources, or if there is resistance to the job or work analysis under way. What adds to cost is the additional time the job analyst spends organizing notes and actually writing the job description or a thorough workflow study. However, the benefits from accurate job descriptions, improved quality, cost savings, efficiency and enhanced communication often far outweigh the costs involved in the interview method.

Questionnaires

When many jobs are to be analyzed, questionnaires often are used in place of interviews. Questionnaires are interviews on paper. They set forth a list of questions that attempt to capture the same information that would be pursued in a one-on-one interview.

Questionnaires are flexible because they can be tailored to the job population being analyzed, especially when the nature of the work is very different. For example, a questionnaire for production jobs most likely would be modified for professional jobs and further modified for executive-level jobs. Such questionnaires are great devices for preparing a job incumbent for an interview. By sending the incumbent a questionnaire a week or so ahead of the actual interview, the chances of a successful interview are increased greatly because the incumbent has a chance to think through the questions and to gather relevant materials.

Frequently, when there are a number of incumbents (positions), analysts will select a sample of individuals to interview after they have received the completed questionnaires. Often, a manager will help the analyst in deciding whom to interview. Usually, it is best to interview the most experienced job incumbents, and the best performers. A combination of completed questionnaires and selective interviewing can be a highly effective way of conducting a thorough job analysis, and it can provide the analyst with a solid basis for developing an accurate and complete job description or a thorough workflow study.

Open-Ended Questionnaires

There are essentially two types of questionnaires. For most professional, managerial and executive level jobs, an "open-ended" questionnaire is appropriate. It is called open-ended because the questions are structured to allow the job incumbent much latitude in responding — the same technique as used during an interview. The questionnaire form should provide a sufficient amount of blank space for job incumbents to complete their answers. (For an example, see Figure 8.)

The responses to open-ended questionnaires may be inadequate for a complete job analysis. Frequently, it is necessary to follow up with the job incumbent to clarify or elaborate on responses; this process can be handled easily over the phone.

FIGURE 8: **POSITION-ANALYSIS QUESTIONNAIRE**

NAME _____ DATE _____

JOB TITLE _____ DEPARTMENT _____

DIMENSIONS Describe any specific measures of your job responsibilities (e.g., budget accountability, operating revenues, number of customers, geographic areas of responsibility, assets under management, etc.)

ORGANIZATION CHART

Your job title

Job titles reporting to you

Indicate the primary function of each area below

DUTIES AND RESPONSIBILITIES Please group your job duties into major areas of responsibility and list them, in order of importance, beginning with the most important.

% time required	Major areas of responsibility

(Attach any additional information you believe is relevant.)

CONTACTS

A. With what other jobs in the company do you have regular contact, and what is the purpose of these contacts?

B. Describe the nature and purpose of any external contacts required by your job.

C. From where do your work assignments come, and where or to whom do you send completed work?

EFFICIENCY AND QUALITY

A. What tasks should be completed before work comes to you?

B. How can work flow be improved?

C. What specific value do you add to the quality of the product or service?

DECISION-MAKING

A. List any formal guidelines, technical manuals, regulations, etc., with which you must comply in fulfilling your job responsibilities.

B. What issues would you refer to your boss before you took any action?

C. What do you consider to be the major challenge(s) of your position?

JOB SPECIFICATIONS — Summarize the specific knowledge, skills and abilities your job requires. (If you were recruiting to fill a job identical to yours, what background would you expect a successful job applicant to have?)

1. Knowledge of:

2. Skill in:

3. Ability to:

4. Describe any previous work experience required to perform your job.

POSITION OBJECTIVE — In one or two sentences, answer the question: "Why does my job exist?" (Focus on end results.)

Approved: _____
Manager

Date _____

Reviewed: _____
Corporate Compensation

Date _____

If the majority of the incumbents in the job population being analyzed have weak language and writing skills, their responses will be of limited value. This is why open-ended questionnaires often are not used for lower-level jobs. On the other hand, highly creative incumbents may enhance responses so the analyst believes their jobs have a much greater impact on organizational success than they actually do, or the analyst may not notice redundancies or inefficiencies.

Closed-Ended Questionnaires

Closed-ended questionnaires, which focus mainly on the frequency of tasks or responsibilities, typically are used for lower-level, production-type jobs. They measure simply whether an incumbent has responsibility for performing a certain task and, if so, how frequently. Two sample questions from a closed-ended questionnaire are shown in Figure 9.

FIGURE 9: CLOSED-ENDED QUESTIONNAIRE

Job-related experience required for competent performance of this job. (Check one.)

- ☐ No experience required
- ☐ Up to one month
- ☐ Over 1 month, up to 12 months
- ☐ Over 1 year, up to 3 years
- ☐ Over 3 years up to 5 years
- ☐ More than 5 years

Maintain effective customer relations. (Check one.)

- ☐ Not part of job
- ☐ Little time spent performing this task
- ☐ Moderate time spent performing this task
- ☐ Substantial time spent performing this task
- ☐ Little time spent supervising this task
- ☐ Moderate time spent supervising this task
- ☐ Substantial time spent supervising this task

Source: Materials for WorldatWork Certification Course C2: "Job Analysis, Documentation and Evaluation"

Closed-ended questionnaires are often designed to be analyzed by computers. The mere fact that a worker does or does not perform a task usually does not address the issues an analyst is trying to uncover in a work-study. The analyst's goal is to improve efficiency and quality, and questionnaires generally are considered to be of limited use in workflow analysis.

There are highly sophisticated closed-ended questionnaires tailored to specific organizations, and some questionnaires are very effective for job evaluation for most levels in an organization because they are behavioral- rather than task-based. These questionnaires are very expensive to develop, and they are processed using computers and statistical techniques. They, too, do not lend themselves to work flow analysis.

Questionnaires: Advantages and Disadvantages

Because the questionnaire method can be used to analyze large numbers of jobs in the least amount of time, it is considered the most efficient method of single-job analysis. However, questionnaires by themselves often result in incomplete, confusing or insufficient answers. If the language and writing skills of the population are inadequate, the results will be weak. If the job population being studied includes employees who do not read or write English, the English version of the questionnaire will have to be translated and the answers interpreted, adding to the cost.

Using questionnaires may be a necessary step, but it probably will not be a sufficient step in documenting work for purposes of a quality study. Follow-up interviews, most likely technical interviews, will be required.

7

Document the Analysis

W hen data gathering is complete, job documentation already has been created, regardless of the data-collection method or combination of methods used. Notes taken during an observation or an interview are a form of job documentation, as are completed questionnaires.

Job descriptions are the most common, complete and usable form of job documentation because they attempt to record the important aspects of a job in an organized, narrative fashion. (See Figures 10, 11 and 12 on pages 40, 41 and 42.) Because job descriptions vary from organization to organization, there is no widely agreed-upon format. However, descriptions usually contain the following sections:

- **Heading:** Important organizational information is provided here (e.g., title, department, FLSA status, current date, job incumbent, reporting relationships, job analyst, etc.).

- **Job Summary:** Two to four sentences usually are written to answer a single question: "Why does this job exist?" It is advisable to write the job summary only after the rest of the job description has been written and the entire job — including the required knowledge, skills and abilities — has been "thought through."

- **Principal Duties:** This section lists the major duties and responsibilities of the job incumbent. It can be organized a number of ways: from the most important responsibility to the least important, most time spent to least time spent, or in order of sequence. For lower-level jobs, it is a good idea to indicate the percentage of time spent on each responsibility, making sure the percentages, of course, total 100.

  Because of the ADA, "principal duties" should be divided into two subsections: essential functions and nonessential functions. Many organizations include a disclaimer statement such as, "Performs other duties as required." This type of disclaimer becomes particularly important as organizations expand the content of jobs and provide more lateral experiences for job incumbents. In a union environment, however, the disclaimer statement might not be permitted, and under the ADA it should pertain only to nonessential functions.

- **Working Conditions:** The physical environment in which the work is performed is described here. Adverse environmental conditions such as noise, heat and fumes are detailed along with the frequency of exposure. Most professional and executive job descriptions do not include this section because work is assumed to be performed under normal office conditions. If it is not, the section should be included.

- **Job Specifications:** Commonly referred to as hiring or background requirements, job specifications tell the reader what specific knowledge, skills and abilities a worker needs to perform the job at a satisfactory level. Avoid simply stating, "B.A. or B.S. required." Instead, list the specific areas of knowledge the incumbent must have, and then conclude (if it is reasonable to do so) that what is listed is "equivalent to a B.A. or B.S." in a specific subject area.

Use the financial analyst job as an example. A specification might read as follows: "This position requires knowledge of accounting, financial analysis and forecasting techniques, as well as quantitative methods acquired through formal education and two to three years of on-the-job application. Also required is computer proficiency in spreadsheet software and word processing, and strong writing and verbal skills to prepare management reports and presentations. Equivalent to a B.A. or B.S. in finance or business administration."

If the objective of the analysis is the "big picture," it probably will be necessary to submit a work-study report. The format of such a report will, of course, depend on management's preferences and the person preparing the report. A work-study report usually includes the job descriptions in an appendix, but the body of the report will describe the work flow, opportunities for improvement, quality pitfalls, inefficiencies and staffing redundancies or inadequacies. Diagram the work flow and highlight the opportunities for improvements. If appropriate, include recommended team rosters.

JOB TITLE: Human Resources Manager

REPORTS TO: Director of Human Resources
JOB INCUMBENT: J. Doe
LOCATION: ABC Division
DATE: January
JOB ANALYST: VCW

JOB SUMMARY

This position is accountable for managing the implementation of human resource policies and practices, programs, processes and procedures for three sites affecting approximately 600 employees, under the direction of the Director of Human Resources, consistent with corporate policies and procedures.

DIMENSIONS: Employee Relations Administrators (3)
Recruiter (1)
Personnel Assistant (2)
Secretary (1)
Employees (600)

1. Provides direction to Employee Relations Administrators to ensure accurate, equitable implementation of human resource policies and procedures.

2. Reviews policies, procedures and education programs provided by corporate headquarters; educates managers and establishes communication programs for employees.

3. Oversees personnel file maintenance for division, including processing of salary increases, job changes, terminations and other personnel actions. Ensures integrity of human resources database information.

4. Provides advice and counsel to division managers concerning employee relations, hiring, progressive discipline, termination, promotions, workers compensation and other human resource actions.

5. Manages recruiting effort for new/replacement jobs to ensure openings are approved, managerial strategy is determined, job is described properly and appropriate recruitment sources are used. Oversees orientation of new employees.

6. Ensures proper termination procedures are followed regarding employees leaving the company.

7. Provides accurate, timely demographic information to corporate, including employment statistics for Affirmative Action programs.

8. Coordinates with Division Safety Manager to maintain safe, productive employee environment.

9. Works with corporate training staff to develop and implement managerial and employee training programs.

10. Develops, recommends and implements employee welfare programs such as stress management, health screenings, etc., and employee activities such as the company picnic, intramural sports leagues and entertainment discounts.

JOB SPECIFICATIONS

Knowledge
Requires English written and verbal communications knowledge; general knowledge of business operations; sufficient employment law, employee relations, and personnel policy knowledge to advise managers; and sufficient knowledge of basic salary administration and benefits programs to ensure accurate implementation.

Skills and Abilities
Strong interpersonal skills to counsel managers and employees, and the ability to communicate effectively in verbal and written form to keep employees and managers apprised of current human resource programs and employee relations issues.

Ability to collect, analyze and interpret statistical data to make recommendations to management regarding utilization of human resource programs.

Ability to manage and develop subordinates.

Ability to travel to three separate locations at least weekly and extend work day into second-shift hours as needed. Ability to respond to emergency calls from second shift at each location.

Knowledge and skills identified above typically are acquired through undergraduate-level studies in human resources, industrial psychology or business administration and five years' progressively responsible human resources experience, including six months with the company for knowledge of company-specific plans and programs.

DISCLAIMER
This job description indicates the general nature and level of work expected of the incumbent. It is not designed to cover or contain a comprehensive listing of activities, duties or responsibilities required of the incumbent. Incumbent may be asked to perform other duties as required.

Approved: _____
Director of Human Resources
Date _____

Reviewed: _____
Corporate Compensation
Date _____

JOB TITLE:	Department Secretary

REPORTS TO:	Controller
JOB INCUMBENT:	S. Jones
FLSA:	Nonexempt
DATE:	January
JOB ANALYST:	VCW

JOB SUMMARY

This position is accountable for providing secretarial support to the Corporate Controller and the department professional staff, including routine and specialized secretarial services.

PRINCIPAL DUTIES

1. Transcribes machine-recorded dictation involving general business vocabulary or a limited range of specialized accounting terminology.

2. Uses word processing software to produce correspondence, reports, tables, financial schedules, etc., from rough drafts, and edits grammar, punctuation or spelling.

3. Assembles and completes a variety of routine reports for approval by Controller, posts data to records and logs, and maintains established files.

4. Responds to routine inquiries from telephone callers and visitors, redirecting calls or providing routine information requiring a detailed knowledge of department functions.

5. Performs routine administrative functions, such as responding to inquiries with a standard letter or arranging meetings and conferences.

6. Maintains Controller's calendar, schedules appointments as directed and arranges travel schedules, as necessary.

7. Sorts, opens and distributes mail directed to department.

8. May take and produce minutes of department meetings.

9. Performs other duties as required.

JOB SPECIFICATIONS

1. Work requires written communication skills to edit and proofread business correspondence and reports.

2. Work requires the ability to type accurately and efficiently from rough draft and machine transcription involving a standard business vocabulary or a limited range of specialized, recurrent accounting terminology using word-processing software.

3. Work requires a thorough knowledge of department policies, practices and operations, and oral communication skill to perform routine administrative duties such as arranging meetings, responding to routine inquiries from telephone callers or visitors, and gathering background information for routine reports.

4. Work requires the ability to analyze routine administrative details of limited complexity such as resolving minor scheduling conflicts, redirecting mail, etc.

5. Work requires ability to read and concentrate via typing and proofreading activities, including numbers, up to 50 percent of time.

6. Work is typically sedentary, but may require standing and walking for up to 10 percent of work time; occasional bending and stooping while accessing files.

The above knowledge and skills normally are acquired through completion of a high school education, plus a two-year vocational office education program or equivalent work experience and nine months related company experience, in addition to one month on-the-job training.

DISCLAIMER

This job description indicates the general nature and level of work expected of the incumbent. It is not designed to cover or contain a comprehensive listing of activities, duties or responsibilities required of the incumbent. Incumbent may be asked to perform other duties as required.

Approved: _____
Controller

Date _____

Reviewed: _____
Human Resources

Date _____

Updated _____

TITLE: Human Resources Manager

TEAM: Human Capital Team
LOCATION: ABC Division
DATE: January
JOB ANALYST: VCW

TEAM OBJECTIVE

The objective of the Human Capital Team is to ensure that appropriate human resources strategies are in place to maximize the division's human capital in support of the business plan.

HR MANAGER TEAM RESPONSIBILITIES

1. Analyzes and determines skills and abilities of existing work force vis-á-vis the five-year business plan and recommends staffing and development strategies to meet the human capital needs of the division.

2. Advises team on training and development needs of the work force, including the cost-benefit analysis of developing and conducting training in-house vs. engaging outside sources.

3. Develops staffing strategies to meet the division's labor needs.

4. Develops compensation strategies that support the business plan.

5. Serves as knowledge expert regarding HR policies, procedures and practices, and recommends revisions as appropriate to support business objectives.

6. Advises team on applicable local, state and federal employment-related statutes.

TEAM MEMBER SPECIFICATIONS

Requires the ability to interpret five-year business plans into human capital needs and to develop appropriate strategies to meet those needs and knowledge of company human resources policies, practices and procedures. Knowledge and skill are usually acquired through undergraduate-level studies in human resources, industrial psychology or business administration and five years of progressively responsible human resources experience.

8

Obtain Necessary Approvals

No job description is complete without the review and approval of the immediate supervisor. If the organization culture supports it, have the job incumbent review a first draft for accuracy, and then submit the revised version to the supervisor for review and approval. Have the supervisor sign and date the description.

Job documentation should be anchored in time so future readers will know exactly when the analysis was done. If someone other than a trained job analyst prepared the job description, have the human resources department review it for content and format consistency. Most organizations require human resources review of the job description.

Obtaining approval for a work-study report might not be straightforward because the recommendations might point to perceived failures on the part of some departments. However, if the whole initiative was positioned as a team effort with substantial participation from line managers and workers, then the final recommendations (Step 11) should be everyone's, not just those of the report's author.

9

Test for Legal Compliance

After summarizing the observation or interview notes — or obtaining a completed questionnaire — ask some questions. Are the job specifications defensible? Does the job content described support the knowledge, skills and abilities required? Will the job content pass an exemption test under the FLSA?

Throughout the observations and interviews, be aware of equipment or processes that would prohibit a disabled person from performing a particular activity, and determine if that activity is "essential" to the performance of the job. Ask whether the activity is necessary to achieve the end result(s) of the job, or whether it is an "add-on" activity that easily could be reassigned to another worker. While going through this analysis, think of ways a disabled worker could perform the activity with the aid of special equipment or with a schedule change.

If appropriate, have the individual responsible for plant safety review the documentation for compliance with the Occupational Safety and Health Act (OSHA). Also, if the final product is a work-study report that recommends substantial organizational changes affecting people's jobs — especially if it results in staff reductions — the EEO specialist should conduct a population analysis to determine if any adverse impact will result from implementation of the recommendations.

10

Conduct a Reality Test

In addition to testing the job documentation for legal considerations, it is always a good idea to step back and look at the big picture. Even if the specific mission was only to analyze single jobs and write job descriptions, a good job analyst always questions the work design to identify opportunities for improvement. Are the analyzed jobs designed to meet departmental objectives identified in the secondary sources? Is the flow of work consistent with meeting those objectives efficiently? Are the right workers interacting regularly to ensure quality? Would establishing a team approach greatly improve efficiency? Is there any duplication of effort? Are there enough quality checkpoints? Are roles and responsibilities defined clearly? Do all workers understand their jobs? Are expectations communicated clearly? Are accountabilities understood? Does everyone in the process take ownership of the end result?

These are just sample questions. More specific questions, depending on the goal of the study, also might be required. The ultimate objective is to realize the maximum from efforts to analyze individual jobs and to examine workflow. The most important question is: What specific suggestions or recommendations can be made to management that would improve quality and efficiency, enhance communications, expedite work flow, reduce costs, empower workers, and so on?

11

Formulate Specific
Recommendations
(Optional)

I f the analyst's role was limited to single-job analysis for the purposes of job evaluation, Step 11 is not required. However, if the end product is a work-study report, organize the opportunities identified in Step 10 into a final report to the appropriate member of management. Include work flow charts and final job descriptions or team rosters to illustrate recommendations.

12

Keep Up to Date

The world is changing constantly. New technology, new products, new markets and reorganizations make existing job documentation obsolete quickly.

Organizations become bureaucracies when old methods and processes become entrenched. Consequently, these methods and processes need to be reviewed much more frequently than in the past. Initially, the task of conducting job and work analysis and creating job documentation is onerous. However, a comprehensive analysis of all jobs does not need to be repeated every time the organization changes. If a procedure is established for keeping job descriptions and other forms of documentation up to date, a total reconstruction of the job-documentation library is not necessary. Establish a "tickler" file that ages job descriptions so that every two or three years a job description (or questionnaire) can be sent to the incumbent and supervisor for review and comment. Many organizations ask managers and subordinates to review job descriptions annually as performance reviews are conducted. This approach serves the dual purpose of updating the description and focusing both parties on appraising performance on the basis of job responsibilities.

Organizations are reorganizing and creating new jobs continually, and managers frequently approach the human resources department for job re-evaluation. As these events occur, job documentation should be updated. With the powerful word processing capability that exists today, keeping job descriptions or questionnaires up to date is not as burdensome as it was in the past. Also, there are many software packages on the market that are designed to facilitate the job description and questionnaire process.

When reorganizations occur, processes change, new technology is introduced or new products are added, the work-study should be updated so opportunities for efficiency and improved quality are not missed. Even if there is no major change, follow-up studies should be scheduled to ensure that the efficiencies and quality improvement initially predicted are occurring.

Job and Work Analysis: Weighing Costs and Benefits

Having a system for managing the job documentation library will ensure that an organization is on top of job and work analysis, and it will strengthen further the organization's position should it be challenged on the employment-law front. Good job documentation, however, is not simply a preventive measure. It also greatly assists an organization's efforts to achieve efficiency and quality, and it facilitates the creation of an equitable job-worth hierarchy. Furthermore, job documentation is used in many other initiatives: hiring, training and development, and succession planning, for instance.

Work analysis provides the basis for quality management programs to assess where processes need to be improved through a change in human behavior such as a job redesign an incentive program, or training in new/enhanced competencies. It also helps determine where processes can be eliminated or streamlined. The review should take place at the individual job level, within a department and across functional lines, and it should follow the product or service from raw material to customer usage. In addition, work analysis can assist an organization to determine if certain elements of the work flow should be considered for "outsourcing" to increase productivity and/or reduce cost.

Initially, job or work analysis appears to be a monumental undertaking, but if approached in an organized way, the effort can yield a tremendous return to the organization over the long term. Perhaps the most important benefit is in improved communications: Job or work analysis can help translate an organization's strategic plan into specific roles and responsibilities.